THE GREAT LITTLE
PUMPKIN
COOKBOOK

by Michael Krondl

CELESTIALARTS
Berkeley, California

CELESTIAL**ARTS**

P.O. Box 7123
Berkeley, CA 94707
e-mail:order@tenspeed.com
website:www.tenspeed.com

Celestial Arts books are distributed in Canada by Ten
Speed Canada, in the United Kingdom and Europe by
Airlift Books, in South Africa by Real Books, in Australia
by Simon & Schuster Australia, in New Zealand by Tan-
dem Press, and in Southeast Asia by Berkeley Books.

Text design by Greene Design
Cover photo by Lois Ellen Frank

Printed in Singapore

Library of Congress Catalog Card Number:
94-12045

1 2 3 4 5 6 7 8 9 10 / 08 07 06 05 04 03 02 01 99 98

CONTENTS

INTRODUCTION

Americans love pumpkins, and it's no wonder—pumpkins, like all squashes, are home grown, all-Americans. They're in the cucurbitaceae family, just like their distant relatives, cucumbers, melons, and gourds, and their kissing cousins, the squashes. Pumpkins are usually one of four species, all of the genus *Cucurbita*. The big orange thing that grows in New England is a *C. pepo*; the tan-colored cheese pumpkin is closely related to butternut squash and belongs to the species *C. moschata*; in the Southwest they call *C. argyrosperma*, like the Green Striped Cushaw, a pumpkin even though it looks more like a zucchini on steroids; and finally there is the *C. maxima*, beloved of giant pumpkin contest winners everywhere.

No matter whether it comes from your garden, a farm stand, or even a can, whether it's cut out to be a fearsome porch ornament, an ingredient in exotic stew, or plain old pie, you know it'll carve a grin on your face. It does on mine. I just love pumpkins.

STARTING WITH SOUP

PUMPKIN APPLE SOUP

2 tablespoons butter or canola oil

1/2 cup coarsely chopped onion

1 1/2 pounds pumpkin, peeled, seeded, and coarsely diced (about 4 cups)

1 tart apple, peeled, cored, and coarsely diced

5 cups chicken broth, homemade or canned low-sodium

2 tablespoons tomato paste

1/2 teaspoon dried thyme leaves

1 bay leaf

Salt and white pepper to taste

Apple slices for garnish

Heat the butter or oil in a large nonreactive saucepan over moderate heat. Add the onion and sauté until softened, about 5 minutes. Add the pumpkin and apple and cook, stirring frequently, about 2 to 3 minutes.

Add the broth, tomato paste, thyme, and bay leaf. Simmer over low heat until the pumpkin is very soft, about 30 minutes. Remove the bay leaf.

Ladle the soup into a blender and purée. Return it to the saucepan and add salt and pepper to taste. Add a little more chicken broth if the soup seems too thick. Garnish with a thin slice of apple.

Serves 6

3

The easiest way to peel a pumpkin, or any hard-skinned winter squash, is to cut it in half and scoop out the seeds and all the stringy bits. Then cut the pumpkin into 2- to 3-inch-wide slices. Place these cut side down on a cutting board and use a large, sharp knife to cut away the skin. Store cut-up pumpkin up to 4 days in the refrigerator.

WHITE BEAN SOUP WITH PUMPKIN AND CHIPOTLE CHILES

1/2 pound cannelini or Great Northern
  beans
1 smoked ham hock, split
1/2 teaspoon dried epazote (optional;
  available in Hispanic markets)
1 to 2 chipotle chiles, dried or en
  adobo
2 tablespoons peanut oil
1 large onion, finely chopped
4 garlic cloves, minced
1 1/2 pounds pumpkin, seeded, peeled,
  and cut into 1-inch cubes
1 small bunch Swiss chard, chopped
1/2 teaspoon dried oregano
1/2 teaspoon salt
Salt and black pepper to taste

Place the beans in a medium bowl, cover with 4 cups of cold water, and let sit overnight.

Drain the beans and transfer to a large saucepan. Add the ham hock and the epazote and cover with 10 cups of water. Bring to a boil, then simmer over low heat until the beans are tender, about 45 minutes.

If the chipotles are dry, cut them in half, place in a small bowl, cover with boiling water, and let sit 30 minutes. Remove the stem and seeds and chop finely. The chiles en adobo need not be soaked, but remove stems and seeds and chop finely.

In a medium skillet, heat the oil over moderately high heat. Add the onion and garlic and sauté until soft. Do not let the garlic brown.

Add the onion mixture to the cooked beans. Add the pumpkin, chard, chiles, oregano, and 1/2 teaspoon salt. Simmer over low heat until the pumpkin is tender, about 20 minutes. Remove the ham hock and add salt and pepper to taste.

Serves 6 to 8

Starting with Soup

CHESTNUT AND PUMPKIN SOUP

1 pound fresh pumpkin (see below) or
   1 cup canned solid pack pumpkin

1/2 pound chestnuts

1 tablespoon butter

1/4 cup chopped onion

1/4 cup chopped celery

1/4 cup chopped carrot

4 cups beef broth, homemade or
   canned low-sodium

1 bay leaf

1/2 cup crème fraiche or heavy cream

Salt and white pepper

Snipped fresh chives for garnish

 *To cook fresh pumpkin:*

Preheat oven to 350°F.

Wrap about 1 pound of pumpkin in aluminum foil. Place on a tray, cut side up, and bake until soft, about 1 hour. Scoop out the flesh and measure 1 cup. Alternatively, use canned solid pack pumpkin.

Using a serrated knife, slit the skin of each chestnut. Bring about 3 cups of water to a rapid boil and add the chestnuts. Boil for 10 minutes. Drain the chestnuts and, using a small paring knife, remove both the exterior shell and the interior skin. (The hotter the chestnuts are, the easier they are to peel.)

Heat the butter in a medium saucepan over moderate heat. Add the onion, celery, and carrot and sauté until softened, about 5 minutes. Add the chestnuts, broth, and bay leaf. Bring to a boil, then simmer over low heat until the chestnuts are very tender, about 20 to 30 minutes. Remove the bay leaf.

Ladle the soup into a blender, add the pumpkin, and purée. Return to the saucepan, add the cream, and bring to a simmer. Season with salt and pepper to taste. Add more broth if the soup seems too thick.

Garnish each serving with a pinch of fresh chives.

Serves 4

SEPHARDIC PUMPKIN AND CHICKPEA SOUP

⁂ This filling soup originated in Morocco, where it has traditionally been served by Sephardic Jews for Rosh Hashanah (the Jewish New Year).

3 tablespoons olive oil

2 medium onions, finely chopped

2 pounds pumpkin, peeled, seeded, and cut into 1-inch dice (5 to 6 cups)

3 cups cooked chickpeas (or two 15-ounce cans, drained)

2 tablespoons honey

6 cups beef broth, homemade or low-sodium canned

2 tablespoons tomato paste

1/2 teaspoon ground cumin

Salt and white pepper

2 tablespoons chopped fresh cilantro

2 teaspoons harissa (hot pepper paste available in specialty stores), or a dash of Tabasco

8

🐾 Heat the oil in a large saucepan over moderate heat. Add the onions and sauté until golden, about 10 minutes. Add the pumpkin, chickpeas, and honey, and sauté for 5 minutes longer.

Add the beef broth, tomato paste, cumin, salt, and white pepper to taste. Bring to a boil and skim off any scum that forms on the surface. Simmer over low heat until the pumpkin begins to fall apart, about 45 minutes. Stir in the cilantro and harissa. Adjust seasoning. Serve with crusty peasant bread or lightly toasted pita bread.

Serves 6 to 8

MAKING PRETTY WITH PUMPKINS
Pumpkins make great containers for soups, salads, dips, cranberry sauce, or pumpkin ice cream. As vases, they're especially pretty when filled with autumn flowers. Miniatures can be hollowed out and used as votive candle holders. In parts of the South, little pumpkins are painted with ghoulish faces and hung from trees.

SUMMER GARDEN SOUP

2 tablespoons olive oil

16 to 24 pumpkin or squash
 blossoms

1 small onion, chopped

2 garlic cloves, chopped

4 cups chicken broth, homemade or
 canned low-sodium

1 pound tomatoes, peeled, seeded,
 and diced

Kernels from 1 ear corn

2 tablespoons fresh chopped cilantro

1 small jalapeño, chopped fine

2 tablespoons lime juice

Salt and pepper

1 avocado, peeled and diced

Heat the olive oil in a large saucepan over moderately high heat. Add the blossoms and sauté until just wilted, 2 to 3 minutes. Remove from the pan and set aside. Add the onion and garlic to the pan and sauté until translucent and soft, about 5 minutes. Add the chicken broth, bring to a boil, then lower the heat and simmer 10 minutes. Add the tomatoes and corn, and simmer 5 minutes.

To serve, stir in the squash blossoms, cilantro, jalapeño, and lime juice. Season with salt and pepper. Spoon into 4 bowls and garnish with the diced avocado.

Serves 4

A NEW ENGLAND SAMPLER

FRESH PUMPKIN PURÉE

Preheat oven to 350°F.

Cut a 9-pound cooking pumpkin into 4 pieces. Scrape out the seeds. Place in a large roasting pan and cover with foil. Cut a few holes in the foil. Place in preheated oven and bake until very soft, about 2 1/2 hours. Remove foil, pour off any liquid, and set aside to cool, uncovered. Scrape the pulp from the peel and purée in batches in a food processor or blender, or pass through a food mill. Line a colander with cheesecloth or coffee filters and set over a large bowl. Spoon the purée into the colander and set aside to drain overnight. A 9-pound cheese pumpkin will yield about 5 cups purée. Refrigerate for up to 5 days, or freeze.

13

PUMPKIN IN A CAN
Homemade pumpkin purée is best, but canned solid-pack pumpkin is 100% pumpkin and it's ready to use. Most of the eating pumpkins Americans grow commercially end up in cans, some 150,000 tons of them. The Libby's Company, grows their own proprietary variety, Libby's Select Dickinson, and has over 80% of the canned market.

PUMPKIN PANCAKES

2 cups all-purpose flour
1 1/2 teaspoons baking powder
1/2 teaspoon baking soda
1 teaspoon pumpkin pie spice
1/4 teaspoon salt
4 tablespoons light brown sugar
3 large eggs
1 2/3 cups buttermilk
3/4 cup pumpkin purée
4 tablespoons butter, melted
Canola oil
Pure maple syrup

SPICE UP YOUR LIFE

Pumpkin pie spice is good not just in pumpkin pie, but in sweet potato pie, apple pie, or apple crisp. Sprinkle some on cereal or a steaming bowl of oatmeal; it does wonders for oatmeal cookies, too. And when you carve that Halloween pumpkin, sprinkle a little on the lid; once you light the candle, the whole house will smell like freshly baked pie.

🍂 Preheat oven to 250°F.

In a large bowl, combine the flour, baking powder, baking soda, pie spice, and salt. Whisk until completely incorporated. In a medium bowl, whisk together the sugar and eggs until well blended. Stir in the buttermilk, pumpkin, and butter. Add the dry ingredients into the wet and whisk until smooth.

Heat a griddle or cast-iron pan over moderately high heat. Brush lightly with oil. Working in batches, drop batter by 1/4 cupsful onto the griddle. Cook pancakes until bubbles form on top and bottoms are golden brown, about 2 1/2 minutes. Turn pancakes over. Cook until bottoms are golden brown, about 2 minutes. Transfer to a baking sheet and place in the oven to keep warm, up to 20 minutes. Repeat with remaining batter, brushing the griddle with oil, as needed.

Serve pancakes hot with maple syrup.

Makes about 12 pancakes, serving 4

PUMPKIN DINNER ROLLS

1 2/3 cups pumpkin purée
4 1/3 cups unbleached all-purpose flour
1 teaspoon active dry yeast
1 tablespoon honey
3/4 cup whole wheat flour
5 tablespoons raw wheat germ (available in natural food stores)
2 teaspoons sea salt
1 teaspoon cumin
1 1/2 cups pumpkin seeds, lightly toasted

In a medium bowl, combine 1/3 cup pumpkin and 1/3 of the flour, then stir in 2/3 cup boiling water. Allow to cool to lukewarm, then stir in the yeast. Cover with plastic wrap and set aside to rise until foamy and bubbling, about 1 hour.

Transfer the yeast starter to a large bowl. Stir in the remaining pumpkin, honey, 1/3 cup cold water, then the remaining all-purpose flour, whole wheat flour, wheat germ, salt, and cumin. Transfer the dough to a floured board and knead until smooth and elastic, about 12 to 15 minutes, adding more flour as necessary. Try not to use any more flour than you need to keep the dough from sticking. Alternatively, use a heavy-duty electric mixer outfitted with a dough hook. Work in the pumpkin seeds.

Place the dough in a lightly oiled large bowl, cover with plastic wrap, and set aside to rise at room temperature until doubled in bulk, about 2 1/2 hours.

Punch down the dough and form into 24 rolls. Set on two cookie sheets lined with parchment. Cover lightly with plastic wrap and set aside in a warm place to rise until doubled in bulk, about 1 1/2 hours.

Preheat oven to 450°F.

Bake the rolls in the center of the oven until puffed and golden, 12 to 15 minutes. Rolls should sound hollow when tapped on the bottom.

Makes 24 rolls

MASHED PUMPKIN WITH ORANGE AND HONEY

2 pounds pumpkin, seeds removed
3 tablespoons butter, cut into small pieces
2 tablespoons honey
1 teaspoon orange rind
Salt

Preheat oven to 400°F.

Place the pumpkin on a baking pan. Cover loosely with aluminum foil. Set in the oven and bake until soft, about 1 hour.

Scrape the cooked pumpkin out of its skin into a sieve and press down with a wooden spoon to extract excess liquid. Transfer to a large bowl and mash the pumpkin with a fork. Stir in the butter, honey, orange rind, and salt to taste.

The mashed pumpkin can be made ahead and reheated in a microwave or 350°F oven.

Serves 4

PUMPKIN CORN BREAD

1/3 cup corn oil
1 cup all-purpose flour
1 cup cornmeal
1 1/4 teaspoons baking soda
1/2 teaspoon salt
1 cup pumpkin purée
1/2 cup buttermilk
2 eggs
2 tablespoons brown sugar

🍎 Brush the inside of a 9- to 10-inch cast-iron skillet with 1 tablespoon of the oil. Place in the oven, then set the oven temperature to 425°F.

In a large bowl, sift together the flour, cornmeal, baking soda, and salt. In a separate bowl, combine the pumpkin, buttermilk, remaining oil, eggs, and brown sugar. Then stir the dry ingredients into the wet until just combined.

Remove the skillet from the oven, pour in the batter, return to the oven, and bake 30 to 40 minutes, until the center is firm. Serve warm in wedges.

Serves 8 to 10

PUMPKIN CORN BREAD STUFFING WITH PUMPKIN SEEDS

1 tablespoon canola oil

3/4 pound Italian sausage, casings removed

1 large onion, chopped

1/2 cup chicken broth, homemade or canned low-sodium

1/2 recipe pumpkin cornbread (see page 18), crumbled, about 5 cups

1/2 cup hulled pumpkin seeds, lightly toasted

1/2 cup dried cranberries

1 teaspoon dried thyme leaves, crumbled

2 tablespoons chopped fresh parsley

Salt and pepper

In a large skillet, heat the oil over medium-high heat. Add the sausage and fry until it is cooked through, breaking it up as it cooks. Using a slotted spoon, transfer the cooked sausage to a large bowl. Drain off all but 2 tablespoons of the fat in the pan. Add the onion and cook over medium heat until the onion is golden and very soft, about 10 minutes. Add the broth and remove from the heat.

To the sausage, add the cornbread, onion with broth, pumpkin seeds, cranberries, thyme, parsley, and salt and pepper to taste. Toss to combine. The mixture should remain a little dry.

Use to stuff a large roasting chicken or turkey. Any additional stuffing can be baked in a separate buttered baking dish, covered with buttered foil. Bake at 350°F until heated through, about 30 minutes. Uncover and bake until top is crisp, about 15 minutes.

Makes about 8 cups dressing, serving 10

TURKEY POT PIE WITH PEAS AND PUMPKIN

You can make this recipe with leftover turkey or chicken—it's terrific both ways.

4 tablespoons butter

1 medium onion, chopped fine

1/3 cup all-purpose flour

1 1/2 cups chicken or turkey broth

1/2 cup heavy cream

1 1/2 pounds pumpkin, peeled and cut into
   1-inch dice, about 4 cups

1 1/2 cups cooked turkey or chicken,
   cut into 1-inch pieces

10 ounces frozen peas

1 tablespoon chopped fresh parsley

1 1/2 teaspoons fresh thyme leaves or
   1/2 teaspoon dried

1 tablespoon lemon juice

1 teaspoon lemon rind

Salt and pepper

1 recipe Single Crust Pie Pastry
   (see page 78)

22

In a medium saucepan, heat 1 tablespoon of the butter over moderately high heat, add the onion, and sauté until soft and transparent, about 5 minutes. Transfer to a large bowl.

In the same pan, melt the remaining butter, stir in the flour, and cook 1 minute. Add the broth all at once and bring to a simmer, whisking continuously. Add the cream and return to a simmer. Remove from heat and set aside.

To the onions, add the pumpkin, turkey, peas, parsley, thyme, lemon juice, and rind. Stir in the sauce. Season with salt and pepper. Set aside to cool to room temperature.

Preheat oven to 400°F.

Spread the turkey-vegetable mixture into an 8-by 11-inch baking pan. Roll out the dough into an 8-by 11-inch sheet and place on top of the filling, tucking the edges against the pan sides. Slash the crust in several places to let the steam escape.

Place on the middle rack of the oven and bake until the bottom is bubbly, the crust is well-browned and the pumpkin tender, about 45 minutes.

Serves 6

APPLE PUMPKIN BUTTER

3 pounds McIntosh apples
2 1/2 cups apple cider
1 1/2 cups granulated sugar
1 cinnamon stick, about 5 inches long
1 3/4 cups pumpkin purée
6 half-pint Mason jars, sterilized
according to manufacturer's
instructions

Peel and core the apples, reserving the peels and cores. Combine the peels and cores in a medium saucepan with 2 cups of the cider. Cover and bring to a boil over high heat, then reduce heat to low and simmer 30 minutes. Strain the juice through a sieve, pressing down on the peels to extract as much juice as possible. Reserve the juice and discard the peels and cores.

While the juice is simmering, combine the apples with the sugar, cinnamon, and remaining 1/2 cup cider in a large, heavy saucepan. Cover tightly and set over medium heat. Bring to a boil, then reduce heat to low and continue cooking, stirring occasionally, until the apples fall apart, 20 to 40 minutes.

Add the reserved juice from the peels to the pan with the apples. With the cover off, raise the heat to medium and continue cooking, stirring occasionally, until the apples are the consistency of thick apple sauce, about 45 to 60 minutes. Remove the cinnamon. Stir in the pumpkin purée.

Preheat oven to 300°F. Pour the apple-pumpkin mixture into a large shallow roasting pan and set in the oven. Keep the oven door slightly ajar. Bake, stirring every 15 minutes, until the mixture is thick enough to spread, 1 to 1 1/2 hours.

Spoon into sterilized preserving jars, leaving 1/2-inch head space. Wipe jar rims and thread clean, top with hot lids, and screw bands on firmly. Process in boiling water 5 minutes. Alternatively, freeze (use freezer jars) after cooling 24 hours. The butter will keep up to 1 month in the refrigerator unprocessed.

Makes about 6 half-pints

SPICED PUMPKIN SEEDS

Preheat oven to 300°F.

Halve or quarter a pumpkin, then scoop out the seeds and rinse them in cold water (they should separate quite easily from the fibrous pulp). Dry the cleaned seeds on a piece of cheesecloth or linen kitchen towel. (An 8-pound pumpkin will yield about 3/4 cup of seeds.) Spread seeds out on a large cookie sheet and bake, stirring every 15 minutes, until the seeds are crisp and lightly browned, about 1/2 hour.

In a bowl, combine each cup of toasted seeds with 2 teaspoons vegetable oil. Sprinkle with 1 teaspoon salt, 1 teaspoon chile powder, 1/2 teaspoon black pepper, and 1/4 teaspoon cumin and toss. Spread out on a baking sheet and bake 10 to 15 minutes longer, until aromatic. Cool and store in an airtight container.

A TASTE OF MEXICO

PUMPKIN BLOSSOM QUESADILLAS

- 2 tablespoons peanut oil, plus oil for the griddle
- 2 tablespoons finely chopped onion
- 1 small clove garlic, chopped
- 1/4 pound pumpkin or squash blossoms, stems removed and blossoms coarsely chopped
- 10 fresh flour tortillas
- 1/2 pound Monterey Jack cheese, grated
- 2 serrano chiles or jalapeños, stems removed and chopped, or to taste

KEEPIN' PUMPKIN

Look for pumpkins without bruises or cuts and with an intact stem. They'll last for a good month at room temperature and up to 3 months in the refrigerator. When stored under ideal conditions, at about 50 degrees and low humidity, they'll make it through Groundhog Day.

🌺 Heat the 2 tablespoons of oil in a large skillet over moderate heat, add the onion and garlic and sauté until just softened. Add the squash blossoms and cook, uncovered, until the blossoms are soft and the liquid from the flowers has evaporated. Set aside to cool.

Heat a griddle or large cast-iron pan and brush lightly with oil.

Place an equal amount of the blossom filling in the center of each tortilla and top with the cheese and chiles. Brush the edge of each tortilla with water and fold in half, pressing the edges to seal.

Fry each quesadilla on the griddle on both sides until golden. Serve warm with guacamole or your favorite salsa.

Makes 10 quesadillas

PUMPKIN STUFFED WITH CHICKEN, CHILES, AND TORTILLAS

 You can easily make this into a satisfying vegetarian dish simply by omitting the chicken.

4 poblano or Anaheim chiles

¼ cup peanut oil

16 corn tortillas

½ pound fresh tomatillos or 1 cup canned tomatillos, drained

½ small onion, coarsely chopped

2 garlic cloves, peeled

10- to 12-pound cheese pumpkin (see page 53)

¼ pound grated Monterey Jack cheese

1 cup sour cream

1 cup cooked chicken or turkey, diced

Salt and freshly ground black pepper

Roast chiles over an open flame until the skins are charred. Place in a plastic bag for 15 minutes, then peel, wash and remove the seeds and stem. Cut into ¹/₂-inch slices.

Heat the oil in a large skillet over medium-high heat. Fry the tortillas on both sides, one or two at a time until they begin to turn golden and crispy, about a minute total. Drain thoroughly on paper toweling. If necessary add a little more oil to the pan. When cool, tear each tortilla into three or four pieces.

If using fresh tomatillos, remove the outer papery layer. Set them in a small saucepan, cover with water, bring just to a simmer, and cook 5 minutes. Drain. In a blender, combine the cooked or canned tomatillos with the onion and garlic. Add a large pinch of salt, and purée.

Preheat oven to 425°F.

Using a sharp knife, and cutting at a slight angle so that the tip of the knife is angled downwards into the vegetable, cut off the top ¹/₄ of the pumpkin to form a lid. With a large spoon, scrape out the seeds.

(recipe continued on next page)

A Taste of Mexico

Fill the pumpkin by beginning with alternating layers of tortillas, green sauce, cheese, sour cream, chiles, chicken, and a generous sprinkle of salt and pepper. Continue layering the tortillas with the other ingredients, finishing with a layer of tortillas. Top with the lid.

Cut a piece of aluminum foil large enough to wrap the entire pumpkin. Brush the pumpkin lightly with oil. Then wrap the pumpkin in the foil and place on a baking pan. Set in the oven and bake about 2 1/2 hours. The pumpkin is done when the skin has softened enough for a sharp knife to easily pierce through to the interior flesh.

Remove from the oven. Carefully remove the foil from the top part of the pumpkin and place the pumpkin on a serving platter. Gently remove the lid. Using a large spoon, stir the interior mixture, making sure to incorporate the pumpkin into the other ingredients. Taste for seasoning and add salt and pepper if necessary. Carefully remove the remaining foil and serve hot.

Serves 8 to 10

PUMPKIN COOKED WITH CHILES AND CREAM

3 poblano or Anaheim chiles
2 tablespoons peanut oil
1 medium onion, finely sliced
1 1/2 pounds pumpkin, peeled and cut into
   1 1/2-inch dice
1/4 cup heavy cream
1/4 teaspoon cumin
Salt and pepper
2 tablespoons hulled pumpkin seeds, lightly toasted

Roast the chiles over an open flame until charred all over. Place in a plastic bag for 15 minutes. Peel, wash, and remove the seeds and stem. Cut into 1/2-inch slices.

Heat the oil in a large, deep skillet over medium heat. Add the onion and sauté until soft and golden, about 10 minutes. Add the chile, pumpkin, cream, cumin, salt, and pepper to taste. Cover and cook until just tender, about 20 minutes, stirring occasionally to prevent sticking. Adjust seasoning. Garnish with the pumpkin seeds.

Serves 4

A Taste of Mexico

PUMPKIN TAMALES WITH SMOKY TOMATO SALSA

The tamales are delicious stuffed with chorizo, but they're equally tasty filled with cooked chicken or with roasted chiles cooked with onions (see page 33 for Pumpkin Cooked with Chiles and Cream).

About 10 large dry corn husks (available in Hispanic markets)

1/2 lb. chorizo sausage, peeled and crumbled or chopped

1 1/2 cups pumpkin purée

1/2 cup lard, cut into pieces

1 teaspoon baking powder

1 teaspoon cumin

Salt

1 1/2 cups masa harina (available in Hispanic markets)

FOR THE SALSA:

1 chipotle chile (use only 1/2 for a mildly spicy sauce)

2 cups drained canned plum tomatoes

2 tablespoons chopped onion

1 garlic clove, chopped

1 tablespoon peanut oil
1 tablespoon chopped fresh cilantro

🌺 Soak the corn husks in hot water for 30 minutes. Tear two of them into 16 thin strips about ¼ inch wide.

In a skillet, fry the chorizo over medium-high heat, until well browned, about 5 minutes.

In a food processor, incorporate the pumpkin, lard, baking powder, cumin, and ½ teaspoon salt. Add the masa and 2 tablespoons water and pulse to form a firm dough.

Lay out the 8 whole husks on a clean work surface. If they are not large enough, overlap 2 smaller ones. Take about ⅓ cup of the dough and spread evenly over each husk, leaving about 1½ inches of exposed husk at each end and 1 inch on each side. Put about 2 tablespoons of the chorizo in the middle of each. Roll up the tamales so that the dough is entirely enclosed in the husks and the edges overlap by at least 1 inch. Twist the ends and tie with the reserved strips of husk.

(recipe continued on next page)

Fill the bottom of a steamer with 2 inches of water. Stand the tamales in the top part of the steamer, cover tightly, and cook until the tamales are firm and the dough comes away easily from the husk, 30 to 35 minutes.

While the tamales are steaming, you can make the salsa. Cut the chile in half lengthwise, place in a small bowl, and cover with boiling water. When soft (about 20 minutes), remove the stem and seeds and chop finely. In a food processor, purée the chile, tomatoes, onion, and garlic. Heat the oil in a small skillet over medium-high heat. Add the tomato mixture and cook at a brisk simmer until thickened, about 8 minutes. Season with salt and add chopped cilantro.

To serve, present the tamales in their husks with the sauce on the side. The cooked tamales may be reheated either by steaming or in a microwave.

Serves 4

YUCATAN-STYLE TACOS WITH TWO SAUCES

¼ cup finely chopped onion
1 tablespoon peanut oil
1½ cups drained canned plum tomatoes, chopped
1 whole habanero or Scotch bonnet chile
Salt and pepper
About 2 cups chicken broth
2 large sprigs fresh epazote or ½ teaspoon dried
   (available in Hispanic markets)
1½ cups hulled pumpkin seeds, lightly toasted
12 corn tortillas
2 cups shredded cooked chicken or pork

🌿 In a small saucepan over medium heat, sauté
the onion in the oil until soft and translucent, about
5 minutes. Add the chopped tomatoes, whole
chile, and salt to taste. Simmer 10 minutes, until
thickened to sauce consistency. Discard the chile
and set aside.

   Combine the chicken broth and epazote in a
medium saucepan and simmer 5 minutes.
Strain the broth and let cool briefly. In a blender,

(recipe continued on next page)

combine the seeds and 1 1/2 cups of the broth and blend until smooth. Add enough broth to make a thin sauce. Return to the saucepan and bring just to a simmer, stirring often. Do not boil. Season with salt and pepper to taste.

To assemble the tacos, heat the tortillas briefly on a griddle or in a cast-iron pan. Dip each tortilla in the pumpkin seed sauce, fill with about 2 tablespoons of the meat, and roll them up. Arrange on a warm serving platter and spoon the tomato sauce over the tacos. Serve warm.

Serves 4 as a main course or 6 as an appetizer

ITALIANS LOVE PUMPKINS TOO

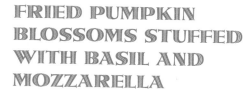

FRIED PUMPKIN BLOSSOMS STUFFED WITH BASIL AND MOZZARELLA

24 large pumpkin or squash blossoms

½ pound mozzarella, cut into 24 chunks (½ by ½ by 2 inches)

24 small basil leaves

½ cup flour, plus additional flour for dusting

½ cup milk

2 eggs, separated

¼ teaspoon salt

Canola or peanut oil for frying

Wash the blossoms, remove their pistils, and dry gently with paper towels. Insert a piece of mozzarella and basil into each blossom so that it is completely enclosed.

In a bowl, mix the ½ cup flour, milk, egg yolks, and salt. In a separate bowl, beat the egg whites until stiff with an electric mixer. Gently fold them into the batter.

Italians Love Pumpkins Too

In a large, heavy saucepan, heat about 2 inches oil to 375°F. Dredge the stuffed blossoms very lightly in flour, dip into the batter, and then carefully place in the oil. Fry in several batches, 3 to 5 minutes, turning once or twice, until golden. Drain on paper towels. Serve immediately.

Serves 4 to 6 as an appetizer

PUMPKIN BLOSSOMS

They're lovely, delicate, and tasty too. Italians stuff and fry them; Mexicans add them to tacos and soups. They are delicious on almost anything from omelettes to pasta. Look for pumpkin or the very similar squash blossoms at farmers' markets and fancy groceries. If you're growing your own patch, you can remove some (but not all!) of the male blossoms. You can tell the difference by the bulge a female blossom has at its base; a male blossom sits on a straight, thin stem. Once all the fruit has set, it's open season on any blossom, boy or girl!

Italians Love Pumpkins Too

SAVORY ITALIAN RICE, SPINACH, AND PUMPKIN TORTE

2 pounds pumpkin, peeled, seeded,
   and coarsely grated (about 3 1/2 cups)
Salt
1/4 cup extra-virgin olive oil
1 medium onion, finely chopped
1 cup rice
Butter
Bread crumbs
3/4 cup cooked spinach, squeezed dry
   and chopped (about 1 pound raw
   spinach)
4 eggs
2 cups grated Parmesan cheese
   (about 6 ounces)
1 teaspoon dried marjoram
1/2 teaspoon freshly ground black
   pepper

42

✂ Place the pumpkin in a colander, sprinkle lightly with salt, and set aside to drain 1/2 hour. Squeeze to extract excess liquid. Heat 1 tablespoon of the oil in a small skillet, add the onion, and sauté until softened, about 5 minutes. Set aside. In a small saucepan, boil 1 cup water, then add 1/4 teaspoon salt and the rice. Simmer over low heat until all the water is absorbed. Set aside.

Preheat oven to 350°F. Butter a 10-inch springform pan and dust the inside with breadcrumbs.

43

Combine the spinach, onion, pumpkin, rice, eggs, Parmesan, marjoram, pepper, and the remaining oil, and season with salt to taste. Spoon into the prepared pan and smooth the top. Bake in the preheated oven until firm and cooked through, about 1 1/2 hours. Let cool before unmolding. Serve warm or at room temperature.

Makes about 12 appetizer portions

FARFALLE WITH PUMPKIN AND PECORINO CHEESE

1 tablespoon olive oil

1/4 pound pancetta, diced (available in Italian groceries and specialty stores)

1 medium onion, finely chopped

2 pounds pumpkin, seeded, peeled, and cut into 3/4-inch dice (about 5 to 6 cups)

1/2 cup chicken broth, homemade or canned, low-sodium

Salt and freshly ground black pepper

1 pound farfalle (bow tie) pasta

2 tablespoons butter or pumpkin oil

1/3 cup grated pecorino romano cheese

3 tablespoons chopped Italian parsley

44

Heat the oil in a large saucepan over medium heat. Add the pancetta and cook until crispy, about 5 minutes. Add the onion and continue cooking until golden, 5 to 7 minutes. Add the pumpkin and chicken broth. Season with salt and pepper to taste. Cover and cook until tender, about 20 minutes. (The recipe can be made ahead to this point.)

To cook the pasta, bring a gallon of water to a boil, then add a teaspoon of salt and the pasta. Cook until just tender, about 10 minutes. Drain the pasta thoroughly, then add it to the pumpkin mixture. Return the mixture to the stove and cook for 3 or 4 more minutes, gently tossing until the liquid is absorbed. Stir in the butter or pumpkin oil, toss with the cheese and parsley, and adjust seasoning. Serve immediately with additional cheese on the side.

Serves 4 to 5

45

CONCHIGLIE STUFFED WITH RICOTTA AND PUMPKIN

1/2 pound large conchiglie (pasta shells)

1 cup pumpkin purée

1 cup ricotta

1 cup grated Parmesan cheese

2 egg yolks

Large pinch nutmeg

Salt and white pepper

1 cup imported Italian mascarpone (see note)

 Cook the conchiglie in plenty of salted boiling water until *al dente*. Drain in a colander and cool under cold running water.

In a medium bowl, combine the pumpkin purée, ricotta, 1/2 cup of Parmesan, egg yolks, and nutmeg. Season with salt and pepper to taste. Fill the shells with this mixture. (The recipe can be made ahead to this point.)

Preheat oven to 375°F. Lightly butter an 8- by 12-inch baking dish. Arrange the stuffed shells in the dish. In a small saucepan, melt the mascarpone over medium heat. Spoon over the shells, and sprinkle with the remaining Parmesan. Cover and bake until the sauce is bubbling, about 25 minutes. Remove the cover and set under a broiler until top is golden brown, 2 to 3 minutes.

Serves 4

Note: If you cannot find imported mascarpone (a very creamy Italian cream cheese), use heavy cream. Domestic mascarpone is made differently and will separate when heated.

PUMPKIN GNOCCHI WITH CRISP-FRIED SAGE LEAVES

1 cup pumpkin purée
1 1/2 cups all-purpose flour
1 cup grated Parmesan cheese
1/2 cup whole milk ricotta cheese
1 egg
1/8 teaspoon nutmeg
Salt
1/4 teaspoon white pepper
Cornmeal
3 tablespoons olive oil
3 tablespoons butter
1/2 cup fresh sage leaves

🍂 In a large bowl, combine the pumpkin, 1 cup flour, Parmesan, ricotta, egg, nutmeg, 1/4 teaspoon salt and white pepper. Stir until smooth. Refrigerate at least 1 hour.

48

To form the gnocchi, generously flour a clean, dry work surface. With generously floured hands, roll the dough into long cylinders about 3/4 inch in diameter. Cut the cylinders with a floured knife at 1/2-inch intervals. Roll lightly in flour and place on trays heavily dusted with cornmeal. The gnocchi should not touch. Refrigerate for up to 2 hours. Freeze for longer storage.

Combine the oil and butter in a medium skillet over medium heat until the butter just begins to color. Add the sage leaves and cook, stirring until they are very crisp and lightly browned. Set aside.

To cook the gnocchi, bring about 1 1/2 gallons water and 1 1/2 teaspoons salt to a gentle boil in a large saucepan. Add the fresh or frozen gnocchi and simmer for 6 to 8 minutes. Carefully remove the cooked dumplings with a slotted spoon and toss with the sage-butter mixture. Serve more Parmesan on the side.

Serves 4

Italians Love Pumpkins Too

PUMPKIN STUFFED RAVIOLI WITH PUMPKIN SEED CREAM

 Making ravioli isn't difficult, but it is time-consuming. A ravioli mold will save you time and make each one perfect.

FILLING:

1 cup pumpkin purée

1 cup (3 ounces) grated Asiago cheese

2 egg yolks

1/4 cup hulled pumpkin seeds, toasted and coarsely chopped

1/4 cup bread crumbs

Large pinch nutmeg

Salt and white pepper

DOUGH:

2 1/4 cups all-purpose flour

3 large eggs

1 tablespoon olive oil

SAUCE:

1/2 cup hulled pumpkin seeds, lightly toasted

3/4 cup heavy cream

Italians Love Pumpkins Too

🍂 *To make the filling:* In a medium bowl, combine the pumpkin, Asiago cheese, egg yolks, chopped pumpkin seeds, bread crumbs, nutmeg, and salt and pepper to taste.

To make the dough: Combine the flour, eggs, olive oil, and ¼ teaspoon salt in a food processor. Process 2 to 3 minutes, until the dough comes together into a ball. Add one or two teaspoons of water if necessary. Gather up the dough and knead briefly by hand. Cover with plastic wrap and allow to rest 10 minutes.

Set smooth rollers of pasta machine on widest setting. Cut the dough in four, lightly flouring each piece. Flatten one piece of dough into a rectangle and feed through rollers. Fold rectangle in half and feed through rollers 4 or 5 more times, folding in half each time and dusting lightly with flour as necessary to prevent sticking. Turn dial down to next (smaller) setting and feed dough through rollers without folding. Continue to feed dough through, without folding, making space between

(recipe continued on next page)

Italians Love Pumpkins Too

51

rollers narrower each time, until narrowest setting is reached and pasta is about 3½ inches wide.

Lay the pasta sheet on a clean, dry work surface with the long side facing you. Place a packed teaspoon's worth of filling 2 inches apart lengthwise along half of the pasta sheet (you should have 10 to 12 mounds). Around each mound of filling, brush dough very lightly with water. Fold dough lengthwise in half over mounds of filling, gently pressing around each mound to force out any air, and seal edges. With a fluted pastry wheel, trim edges and cut between mounds of filling to separate ravioli. Alternatively, use a ravioli mold.

Line a large tray with a dry kitchen towel and arrange ravioli in a single layer. Finish making ravioli with remaining dough and filling and arrange on towel-lined trays in single layers. Ravioli may be made 8 hours ahead and chilled on towel-lined tray, covered loosely with plastic wrap. They can also be frozen.

52

To make the sauce: In a blender, combine the 1/2 cup pumpkin seeds with 1/2 cup water and blend until smooth. In a small saucepan, combine with the cream and season with salt and white pepper. Bring just to a simmer.

To cook the ravioli: Bring about a gallon of water to a boil in a large pan, then add 1 teaspoon salt and the ravioli. Cook 6 to 8 minutes. Drain in a colander and toss with the sauce.

Makes about 4 1/2 dozen ravioli, serving 4 to 5

PICK YOUR PUMPKIN

Most large, pretty pumpkins are bland and watery and best suited for jack-o'-lanterns. The orange cooking varieties such as a "sugar" or "pie pumpkin," weigh about 7 pounds. "Cheese pumpkins" which are beige on the outside have orange meat that's thick and tasty. At 10 to 12 pounds there's plenty for soup, stew and pie. If you can't find a pumpkin, you can substitute winter squash. Hubbard, turban, buttercup, kabocha, or butternut squash all work well.

Italians Love Pumpkins Too

PUMPKINS TRAVEL THE WORLD

PUMPKIN OIL DRESSING

¹/₄ cup balsamic vinegar
2 teaspoons Dijon-style mustard
¹/₄ cup olive oil
¹/₄ cup pumpkin seed oil
Salt and black pepper

In a medium bowl, whisk together the vinegar and mustard. Slowly whisk in the olive and pumpkin seed oils. Season with salt and pepper. Use to dress mixed green salads, spinach salad, or steamed vegetables.

Makes ³/₄ cup

LIQUID GOLD

Only recently available in the U.S., Austrian pumpkin seed oil comes from Styria, a region of Austria where this rich, nutty oil is as common as olive oil is in Italy. You need about 5 pumpkins to make a cup of oil, which is used more like a flavoring than a cooking medium. It's terrific in a vinaigrette, luscious on pasta, and divine on a green salad. Stored in a cool, dark place, it should last about nine months. If you can't locate the oil locally, it can be mail-ordered. One source is Zabar's at (800) 697-6301.

Pumpkins Travel the World

INDIAN PUMPKIN FRITTERS

1 pound pumpkin, peeled, seeded,
and coarsely grated (about 1 3/4 cups)

1/2 cup chickpea flour (available in
Indian and Middle Eastern markets)

1 small onion, peeled and grated,
about 1/4 cup

2 tablespoons chopped fresh cilantro

1 small jalapeño chile, stem removed,
finely chopped, or to taste

1 1/2 teaspoons ground coriander seed

1/2 teaspoon paprika

1/2 teaspoon salt

1/4 teaspoon black onion seeds (available in Indian and Middle Eastern
markets)

1/4 teaspoon baking powder

Peanut oil for frying

56

🍂 In a medium bowl, combine the pumpkin, chickpea flour, onion, cilantro, chile, coriander, paprika, salt, onion seeds, and baking powder.

Fill a deep, heavy saucepan with oil to a depth of about 2 inches and heat to 350°F. With a spoon, form the pumpkin mixture into small balls no larger than 1 inch and drop into the oil. Cook several fritters at a time, making sure not to crowd the pan. Fry about 4 to 5 minutes until well browned, stirring occasionally. Drain on paper towels. Repeat with remaining batter. Serve hot.

🍂 *Note:* The fritters may be kept hot for up to 30 minutes in a 200° oven or reheated in a 300°F oven for about 5 minutes.

Makes about 30 fritters, serving 5 to 6 as an appetizer

NORTH AFRICAN CHICKEN TAGINE

2 tablespoons lemon juice

2 tablespoons olive oil

3 cloves garlic, minced

Salt

1 teaspoon ground ginger

1/2 teaspoon paprika

1/4 teaspoon ground cumin

1/2 teaspoon turmeric

1/4 teaspoon black pepper

3- to 4-pound chicken, cut into 8 pieces

1 medium onion, finely chopped

Large pinch saffron

1 1/2 pounds pumpkin, peeled, seeded, and cut into 1 1/2-inch pieces (about 4 cups)

1 preserved lemon, cut into 8 pieces (available at specialty stores) or 1 teaspoon grated lemon rind

1/2 cup Gaeta or Kalamata olives, pitted

3 tablespoons chopped Italian parsley

58

In a large bowl, combine the lemon juice, olive oil, garlic, ½ teaspoon salt, ginger, paprika, cumin, turmeric, and pepper. Add the chicken and toss. Cover and refrigerate overnight.

Combine the chicken and its marinade with the onion, saffron, and 1 cup water in a flame-proof casserole. Bring to a boil, cover, then lower heat and simmer until the chicken is just barely cooked through, about 30 minutes. Add the pumpkin and continue simmering, covered, until the chicken and pumpkin are cooked through, about 30 minutes longer. Add the pre-served lemon, olives, and parsley and continue simmering 5 minutes.

Arrange the chicken and pumpkin on a warm serving platter. Skim off fat from the cooking juices, if necessary, then bring the juices to a rapid boil and cook until reduced to about 1¼ cups. Adjust the seasonings. Pour over the chicken. Serve with couscous.

Serves 4

Pumpkins Travel the World

PUMPKIN SPANAKOPITA

2 tablespoons olive oil
1 large onion, finely chopped
2 1/2 cups pumpkin purée
4 eggs, lightly beaten
12 ounces feta cheese, crumbled
1/2 cup bulgur wheat
1/4 cup chopped Italian parsley
1/4 teaspoon ground nutmeg
Salt and black pepper
1 pound filo dough
6 tablespoons melted butter

EAT YOUR PUMPKIN

Of course pumpkin is good for you. It's an especially good source of Vitamin A in the form of beta-carotene. A cup of cooked pumpkin provides some 2600 RE of vitamin A, two to three times the recommended daily allowance. Homemade pumpkin puree, as well as canned, have even more. Pumpkin is also low in calories and relatively rich in dietary fiber.

Heat the oil in a skillet over medium heat. Add the onion and sauté until very soft, about 10 minutes. In a large bowl, combine the onion, pumpkin, eggs, feta, bulgur, parsley, nutmeg, ground black pepper, and about 1 teaspoon salt, or to taste.

Preheat oven to 375°F. Lightly butter a 9- by 13-inch baking pan.

Trim the filo dough to 11 by 15 inches. Cover with plastic wrap while working. Lay 1 sheet of filo in and up the sides of the prepared pan and brush lightly with melted butter. Top with 7 more sheets, brushing each one lightly with butter. Spread with the pumpkin mixture. Top with 8 more sheets of filo, brushing each lightly with butter, including the top sheet.

Bake until crisp and golden, about 45 minutes. Remove from the oven and let stand 10 minutes. Cut into 20 squares with a small, sharp serrated knife. Serve warm or at room temperature.

Serves 10

CATALAN PORK, BEAN, AND PUMPKIN STEW

3/4 pound white kidney beans or Great
    Northern beans

2 tablespoons olive oil

2 pounds lean pork shoulder,
    boneless and in one piece

Salt and pepper

1 large onion, finely chopped

4 garlic cloves, peeled and cut in half

1 cup white wine

1 smoked ham hock (about 3/4 lb.), cut
    in half

2 tablespoons tomato paste

2 bay leaves

1/2 teaspoon thyme

1 1/2 pounds pumpkin, peeled and cut
    into 1 1/2-inch pieces

 Cover the beans with 3 cups of water and
soak overnight. Rinse and drain.

Preheat oven to 350°F. Heat the oil in a large
ovenproof Dutch oven or casserole over medium-
high heat. Season the meat generously with salt

and pepper. Brown the pork in the pan on all sides, about 5 to 8 minutes. Remove from the pan, lower heat to medium, add the onion and garlic, and sauté until soft and translucent, about 5 minutes. Add the wine and scrape the bottom of the pan to loosen any browned bits. Replace the pork, add the beans, ham hock, tomato paste, bay leaves, thyme, and $1/2$ teaspoon salt. (Do not omit the salt, otherwise the beans will become mushy!) Cover with $1 1/2$ cups of water. Bring to a boil, cover, set in the oven, and cook 1 hour 45 minutes.

63

Add the pumpkin to the beans and continue cooking for 30 more minutes until the pork and pumpkin are tender.

Remove the pork from the beans and slice. Discard the ham hock and bay leaves. Add salt and pepper to taste.

To serve, place a layer of rice in individual bowls. Arrange pieces of sliced pork in the center and surround with the beans.

Serves 6

ROASTED PUMPKIN STUFFED WITH BREAD AND GRUYÈRE CHEESE

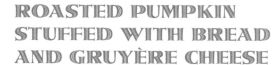

*I learned how to make this fabulous
dish from Alain Senderens, one of
France's renowned three-star chefs.
If you can only find big pumpkins,
increase the filling and cooking time
proportionately.*

1 (5-pound) cooking pumpkin
1/2-pound loaf French or Italian country-style bread
1 cup crème fraiche
6 ounces grated Gruyère cheese
Salt and black pepper
2 tablespoons vegetable oil

Rinse the outside of the pumpkin and wipe dry.
Using a sharp knife, and cutting at a slight angle so
that the tip of the knife is angled downwards into
the vegetable, cut off the top 1/4 of the pumpkin to
form a lid. With a large spoon, scrape out the seeds.
   Cut the bread into thin slices and toast until
golden brown. Set aside.

Preheat oven to 425°F.

Line the pumpkin cavity with one layer of the bread, spread with 4 tablespoons of the crème fraiche, ¼ of the cheese, and a generous sprinkle of salt and freshly ground pepper. Continue layering (4 layers in all), finishing with the Gruyère. Set the top back on the pumpkin.

Cut a piece of aluminum foil large enough to wrap the entire pumpkin. Brush the pumpkin lightly with the oil. Wrap the pumpkin with the foil and place on a baking pan. Set in the oven and bake about 1 hour 40 minutes. The pumpkin is done when the skin has softened and a sharp knife can easily pierce through to the interior flesh.

Remove from the oven, discard the foil, and place the pumpkin on a serving platter. Carefully remove the lid and stir the interior mixture, making sure to incorporate the pumpkin into the other ingredients. Add salt and pepper to taste. Serve hot.

Serves 4 to 6

SWEET AND SOUR SOUTH INDIAN PUMPKIN

1 tablespoon ground coriander
1 teaspoon chopped fresh ginger
2 garlic cloves, chopped fine
Pinch cayenne pepper or to taste
1/4 teaspoon ground black pepper
3 tablespoons canola oil
2 pounds pumpkin, peeled and cut
   into 1 1/2-inch pieces (about 6 cups)
Salt
2 tablespoons lemon juice
3 tablespoons light brown sugar
1 tablespoon chopped cilantro

Pumpkins Travel the World

🌿 Preheat oven to 350°F.

In a small bowl, combine the ground coriander, ginger, garlic, cayenne, and black pepper.

Heat the oil in a large ovenproof casserole over medium heat until hot. Add the spice mixture and cook, stirring until it turns a little darker and is very aromatic, about 1 minute. Do not burn! Immediately add the pumpkin and stir to coat with the spices. Sprinkle with about 1/2 teaspoon salt and cover. Set in the oven and bake until the pumpkin is just barely tender, about 25 minutes.

67

Remove the pan from the oven. Using a slotted spoon, remove the pumpkin pieces. Set the pan over medium-high heat, stir in the lemon juice, and cook, uncovered, for 1 minute. Stir in the brown sugar and cook 3 to 4 minutes until the sugar dissolves and the juices are syrupy. Add the pumpkin and toss. Season with more salt and pepper to taste. Sprinkle with the fresh coriander and serve.

Serves 4 as a side dish

Pumpkins Travel the World

EAST AFRICAN PUMPKIN SWEET POTATO STEW

1 tablespoon peanut oil

1/2 cup finely chopped onion

1 pound (3 to 4 cups) pumpkin, peeled, seeded, and cut into 2-inch pieces

1 pound (3 medium) sweet potatoes, peeled and cut into 2-inch pieces

1 cup canned unsweetened coconut milk

1 tablespoon lemon juice

Salt

4 cloves

1/2 teaspoon cinnamon

Pinch cayenne pepper

1/4 cup peanuts, coarsely chopped

Heat the oil in a large heavy saucepan over medium heat. Add the onion and sauté until translucent and soft, about 5 minutes. Add the pumpkin, sweet potatoes, coconut milk, lemon juice, about 1 teaspoon salt, the cloves, cinnamon and cayenne pepper. Cover and cook at a bare simmer over low heat until the vegetables are tender, about 40 minutes.

To serve, spoon the vegetables into a serving dish and sprinkle with the peanuts.

Serves 4 as a side dish

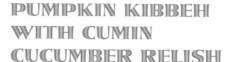

PUMPKIN KIBBEH WITH CUMIN CUCUMBER RELISH

FILLING:

1 tablespoon olive oil

¼ cup pine nuts

¼ cup finely chopped onion

¾ cup cooked, drained spinach, chopped

1 tablespoon lemon juice

Pinch cayenne pepper

Salt and black pepper

SAUCE:

1 cucumber, peeled, seeded, and coarsely grated

1 cup plain yogurt

1 tablespoon lemon juice

1 clove garlic, finely chopped

¼ teaspoon ground cumin

SHELL:

1 1/2 cups fine grain bulgur (tabouli)

1 cup pumpkin purée

1/4 cup flour

1/4 cup finely chopped scallions

1/2 teaspoon ground cumin

Large pinch cayenne pepper

Canola oil, for frying

🐚 To make the filling: Heat the olive oil in a small skillet over medium heat. Add pine nuts and sauté until pale gold. Add the onion and sauté until translucent and soft, about 5 minutes. Stir in the spinach, lemon juice, cayenne, salt, and black pepper to taste.

To make the sauce: Using your hands, squeeze out as much liquid as possible from the cucumber. In a small bowl, combine the cucumber, yogurt, lemon juice, garlic, cumin, and salt to taste.

To make the shell: In a medium bowl, combine the bulgur, pumpkin, flour, scallions, 3/4 teaspoon

(recipe continued on next page)

Pumpkins Travel the World

salt, 1/4 teaspoon black pepper, cumin, and cayenne. Set aside for 10 minutes.

To shape the kibbeh: Moisten your hands and knead about 2 tablespoons of the pumpkin mixture until it holds together. Holding the piece of dough with one hand, use your finger to make a deep hole in the dough. Fill with about 2 teaspoons of filling. Form into a lozenge about 2 1/2 by 1 1/2 inches. Proceed until all the dough has been used up. Cover the formed kibbeh and refrigerate until ready to fry.

In a deep, heavy pan, heat about 2 inches oil to 375°F. Fry 4 or 5 kibbeh at a time, until golden, about 1 1/2 minutes. Drain on paper towels. Serve warm or at room temperature with the sauce on the side.

Makes 16, serving 4 as an appetizer

SWEET AS PIE

TRADITIONAL PUMPKIN PIE WITH HONEY

1 recipe single crust pie pastry (see page 78)
1 cup pumpkin purée
3/4 cup heavy cream
3 large eggs
3/4 cup honey
1 1/2 teaspoons ground cinnamon
2 tablespoons finely chopped candied ginger
1/4 teaspoon ground cloves
1/4 teaspoon grated nutmeg
Large pinch salt
2 teaspoons vanilla extract

VARIATIONS ON A PIE

Be creative: substitute banana purée for half the pumpkin in the filling, use unsweetened coconut milk instead of the cream; top it with meringue; sweeten a pie with maple syrup or raw brown sugar; flavor it with bourbon, rum, Grand Marnier, or amaretto; or decorate it with whipped cream and invite yourself to a pie fight.

Preheat the oven to 400°F.

On a clean, dry, floured work surface, roll out the dough into a 13-inch circle. Carefully transfer to a 9-inch pie pan. Trim and crimp the edges to form a raised lip around the edge of the pie about 1/2 inch high. Cover with aluminum foil and weigh it down with dried beans or pie weights. Set on the bottom rack of the oven and bake 15 minutes. Remove the foil and weights and set aside to cool.

Thoroughly combine the pumpkin with the cream, eggs, honey, cinnamon, ginger, cloves, nutmeg, salt, and vanilla.

Spoon the filling into the partially baked crust.

Place the pie in the bottom third of the oven and bake 8 minutes. Reduce the heat to 350°F and continue baking another 45 to 50 minutes, until the center is firm. Do not overcook!

Serve warm or at room temperature, decorated with whipped cream, if you wish.

Serves 6 to 8

OLD ENGLISH APPLE PUMPKIN PIE

2 recipes single crust pie pastry
  (see page 78)
1 ½ pounds cooking pumpkin
1 pound firm cooking apples such as
  Northern Spy, Baldwin, or Golden
  Delicious
2 tablespoons cider vinegar
3 tablespoons flour
¾ cup dark brown sugar
½ teaspoon cinnamon
Large pinch nutmeg
Large pinch cloves
1 egg, lightly beaten

Roll out half of the pastry for a bottom crust and place in a 9-inch pie pan. Cover and refrigerate.

Preheat oven to 425°F.

Scoop out the pumpkin seeds, then cut the pumpkin into 1-inch strips, cut away the peel, and slice the strips into ⅛-inch-thick pieces (about 4 cups). Peel, quarter, and core the apples. Cut into ¼-inch slices. In a large bowl, toss the pumpkin with the apples, vinegar, flour, sugar, cinnamon, nutmeg, and cloves. Arrange in the pastry-lined pie pan.

Brush the edge of the dough with the beaten egg. Roll out the remaining dough and place on top of the filling. Crimp the edges. Cut vent holes in the top crust and brush the top with the egg.

Set on the bottom shelf of the oven. Bake 20 minutes. Lower temperature to 350°F. and continue baking until golden brown and the pumpkin offers no resistance to a knife or skewer, about 1 more hour. Cool at least 2 hours before serving. Serve at room temperature or slightly warm.

Serves 6 to 8

SINGLE CRUST PIE PASTRY

1 1/4 cups bleached all-purpose flour
1/4 teaspoon salt
4 tablespoons unsalted butter, cut
    into small pieces
3 tablespoons lard or vegetable
    shortening
3 tablespoons ice water

 Sift together the flour and salt. Add the butter and shortening. Using your hands or a pastry cutter, break up the two fats in the flour until the mixture is about as fine as rolled oats. Add just enough water to moisten the flour. Toss to form a rather dry dough. Do not overmix. Gather the dough together and wrap in plastic film. Refrigerate at least 2 hours.

Makes enough dough for 1 single crust pie

PUMPKIN PIE SPICE

4 teaspoons ground cinnamon
2 teaspoons ground ginger
1 teaspoon grated nutmeg
1 teaspoon ground allspice

In a small bowl, combine the spices and store in an airtight container.

Makes 8 teaspoons spice

WHO INVENTED PUMPKIN PIE?

When the Puritans first landed on New England's blustery shore they already knew about pumpkins or "pompions" as they called them. Pumpkins from Central America had been introduced into England years before. Contemporary recipes for "pompion pie" often included apples as well as salt and pepper. It's likely they enjoyed one of these savory pies at the first Thanksgiving. The custard-filled dessert we're used to was developed during the late colonial era, though it used to be called baked pudding, not pie, until little more than a hundred years ago.

CARAMELIZED PEAR PUMPKIN TART

CRUST:

1 1/3 cups all-purpose flour

1/2 cup unsalted butter, cut into small pieces

1 egg

2 tablespoons sugar

1 1/2 tablespoons cold water

FILLING:

1/3 cup blanched almonds

2 tablespoons granulated sugar

2 tablespoons brown sugar

1/3 cup pumpkin purée

1/4 cup heavy cream

1 egg

1/2 teaspoon ground cinnamon

1/2 teaspoon vanilla extract

Pinch salt

4 ripe medium pears, peeled, cored, cut in half, and cut into 1/4-inch slices

3 tablespoons apricot preserves

🍎 *To make the crust:* Combine the crust ingredients in a food processor fitted with a metal blade and process until the mixture forms a mass. If it doesn't form a mass after 25 seconds, add another teaspoon water. Refrigerate until firm, about 1 hour.

Preheat oven to 400°F.

On a floured work surface, roll out dough to fit a 10-inch tart pan. Press into the pan and prick all over with a fork. Cover with aluminum foil and weigh it down with dried beans or pie weights. Set on bottom rack of the oven and bake 12 minutes. Remove foil and continue baking until crust is pale golden, about 10 minutes. Set aside to cool.

To make the filling: In a food processor, grind the almonds and granulated sugar until fine. Add brown sugar, pumpkin purée, cream, egg, cinnamon, vanilla, and salt. Purée and pour into the bottom of the tart pan. Arrange the pears on top. Set in the oven and lower heat to 350°F. Bake until the pumpkin mixture is set, about 45 minutes. Let cool.

In a small saucepan, heat the preserves. Brush all over the top of the tart.

Serves 6

Sweet as Pie

LOW-FAT PUMPKIN PIE

CRUST:

3/4 cup cake flour

1/4 cup all-purpose flour

1 teaspoon sugar

Pinch salt

4 tablespoons butter

2 tablespoons ice water

FILLING:

1 3/4 cups pumpkin purée

1 cup nonfat evaporated milk

1/2 cup maple syrup

1/3 cup light brown sugar

2 egg whites

1 whole egg

1 1/2 teaspoons pumpkin pie spice

1 teaspoon vanilla extract

Pinch salt

82

Preheat oven to 425°F.

To make the crust: In a medium bowl, combine both kinds of flour with the sugar and salt. Cut in the butter until the mixture resembles oatmeal. Sprinkle with the water and stir lightly to blend. Gather into a ball. On floured waxed paper, roll out the dough to a 12-inch round (it will be thin). Transfer to a pie pan and crimp the edges to form a ¼-inch-high border around the edge. Prick the bottom with a fork. Set on the bottom shelf of the oven and cook until very pale gold, about 12 to 15 minutes. Set aside to cool briefly. Lower oven temperature to 350°F.

In a large bowl, combine the pumpkin purée, milk, syrup, brown sugar, egg whites, whole egg, pumpkin spice, vanilla and salt. Whisk until smooth. Pour into the prepared pie shell, set on the bottom shelf of the oven, and bake until the center is firm, about 45 to 55 minutes. Cool on a rack.

Makes 10 servings

SUGAR AND SPICE

PUMPKIN WALNUT BREAD

3/4 cup pumpkin purée
2/3 cup dark brown sugar
1/2 cup walnut oil or other vegetable oil
2 eggs
1 teaspoon vanilla
1 1/3 cups all-purpose flour
1 teaspoon ground ginger
1 teaspoon ground cinnamon
3/4 teaspoon baking soda
1/4 teaspoon salt
1/2 cup coarsely chopped walnuts

🐿 Preheat oven to 350° F. Butter and flour a 4- by 9-inch loaf pan.

In a medium bowl, combine the pumpkin, sugar, oil, eggs, and vanilla until well incorporated. In a separate bowl, sift together the flour, ginger, cinnamon, baking soda, and salt. Combine the pumpkin and flour mixtures just until the two are barely incorporated. Stir in the walnuts. Pour batter into the prepared pan and bake for about 50 minutes or until cooked through.

Makes 1 loaf, serving 8

Sugar and Spice

LOW-FAT PUMPKIN AND OATMEAL MUFFINS

¼ cup walnut oil or other vegetable oil
⅔ cup light brown sugar
¾ cup pumpkin purée
2 egg whites
¾ cup buttermilk
1¼ cups all-purpose flour
1 teaspoon baking soda
1 teaspoon ground cinnamon
1 teaspoon ground ginger
¼ teaspoon grated nutmeg
¼ teaspoon ground cloves
Pinch salt
1¼ cups rolled oats
½ cup seedless raisins

Preheat the oven to 350°F. Lightly spray a 12-muffin tin with non-stick vegetable spray.

In a large bowl, combine the oil and brown sugar. Add the pumpkin, egg whites, and buttermilk and stir until smooth. In a separate bowl,

sift together the flour, baking soda, cinnamon, ginger, nutmeg, cloves, and salt. Combine
the flour mixture with the pumpkin and the oats.
Add the raisins and stir until just mixed. Spoon
into the prepared muffin tins, filling almost to the
top. Bake for about 25 minutes until a toothpick
inserted into the center comes out clean.

Makes 1 dozen muffins

87

HALLOWEEN STORY

All Hallows' Day is an ancient festival that predates
Christianity. The Ancient Celts observed "Samhain"—
part harvest festival, part ancestor worship—with dis-
guised revelers making merry as they carried lanterns
carved from turnips. The ancient Romans celebrated the
goddess Pomona to similar effect. In Mexico, the Day of
the Dead dates back to pre-Columbian days, and is
marked by jack-o'-lanterns and parties in the grave-
yards. In America today, we spend more money on Halloween than any other holiday except Christmas and
throw more parties than any day but New Year's Eve.

HALLOWEEN CUPCAKES

🦇 *Bake in cupcake liners decorated with a Halloween theme. Alternatively, use miniature loaf pans, then decorate to resemble coffins. Color the icing with orange and/or black food coloring. Paste colors work best.*

CUPCAKES:

2 cups all-purpose flour
1 teaspoon baking soda
1 teaspoon ground cinnamon
1/2 teaspoon ground ginger
1/4 teaspoon ground nutmeg
1/4 teaspoon salt
1/2 cup butter, softened
1 cup light brown sugar
2 large eggs
1 cup pumpkin purée
3/4 cup chopped pecans

FROSTING:

4 ounces cold cream cheese
3 tablespoons butter, softened

88

1 tablespoon orange juice concentrate
¹/₄ teaspoon pure orange extract
1¹/₂ cups confectioners' sugar
Food coloring

Preheat oven to 350°F. Spray 12-muffin tin with vegetable spray or line with cupcake liners.

Sift together the flour, baking soda, cinnamon, ginger, nutmeg, and salt. In a separate bowl with an electric mixer, beat the butter and sugar until well incorporated. Beat in the eggs and then the pumpkin. On low speed, beat in the dry ingredients just until blended. Stir in the pecans. Transfer batter to prepared pans, filling each about three-quarters full. Bake until a tester inserted into a cupcake comes out clean, about 30 to 35 minutes. Cool.

To make the frosting: In a medium bowl with an electric mixer, beat the cream cheese and butter just until smooth. Beat in the orange juice concentrate and extract. Gradually beat in the confectioners' sugar. Tint with desired food coloring. Frost and decorate the cupcakes.

Makes 1 dozen cupcakes

Sugar and Spice

PUMPKIN SOUFFLÉ WITH BOURBON CUSTARD SAUCE

Butter
Granulated sugar
2 egg yolks
1/4 cup brown sugar
2 tablespoons flour
1/2 cup heavy cream
1 cup pumpkin purée
1/2 teaspoon vanilla extract
1 teaspoon grated orange rind
1/2 teaspoon cinnamon
Large pinch grated nutmeg
Large pinch ground cloves
4 egg whites
Large pinch cream of tartar
Confectioners' sugar
Bourbon custard sauce (recipe
  follows)

🦂 Preheat oven to 475°F. Butter the inside of a 4-cup soufflé mold and dust with granulated sugar.

Whisk the egg yolks and brown sugar together in a small bowl. Add the flour and mix until smooth.

In a small saucepan, bring the cream to a boil.

Gradually stir the hot cream into the yolk mixture. Return to the saucepan and stir rapidly over moderate heat, making sure to stir the bottom and sides of the pan, until the mixture is very thick and just barely simmering. Remove the pan from the heat, transfer the mixture to a large bowl, and stir in the pumpkin, vanilla, orange rind, cinnamon, nutmeg, and cloves.

In a separate bowl, beat the egg whites with the cream of tartar until they form firm, shiny peaks. Fold one third of the egg whites into the pumpkin mixture, then fold in the remainder. Pour the batter into the prepared mold and level the surface with a spatula.

(recipe continued on next page)

Sugar and Spice

Bake the soufflé on the lowest rack of the oven for 5 minutes. Lower the temperature to 425°F and bake another 5 to 10 minutes, until the soufflé has risen an inch or two above the top of the mold, and is golden brown and springy to the touch.

Dust the top with confectioners' sugar and serve immediately accompanied by bourbon custard sauce.

Serves 4

JACK'S LANTERN

Once there was an Irish lad named Jack who traded his soul to the Devil for one last drink. But Jack was not only a drunkard, he was a cheat too, and managed to evade his bargain with the Evil One. Yet even Jack had to pass on eventually. When he knocked on the Pearly Gates, however, they'd have nothing to do with the likes of him. Out of luck, he next tried hell, but even Beelzebub sent him packing with only a glowing hellish coal to illuminate Jack's way as he wandered aimlessly through the world. To keep this last ember from blowing out, Jack carved a lantern from a turnip, the first jack-o'-lantern.

BOURBON CUSTARD SAUCE

3/4 cup milk
3 egg yolks
3 tablespoons sugar
1/4 cup bourbon
1/2 teaspoon vanilla extract

In a small saucepan, bring the milk to a simmer. In a medium bowl, whisk the yolks together with the sugar. Whisk in the hot milk, then add the bourbon.

Pour into a clean, small saucepan and set over low heat. Cook, stirring continually, until sauce is thick enough to cover the back of a spoon. Stir in the vanilla. Set aside to cool.

Makes 1 cup

PUMPKIN COCONUT FLAN

1/3 cup sugar
1 cup half-and-half
1 cup canned cream of coconut
4 whole eggs
2 egg yolks
1 cup pumpkin purée
1/4 cup rum
1 teaspoon vanilla extract
1/4 teaspoon allspice
1/2 cup sweetened flaked coconut,
   lightly toasted

To make the caramel: Combine 1/4 cup water and the sugar in a small, heavy saucepan. Cook over moderate heat, without stirring, until the sugar turns an amber color. Immediately pour the caramel into an 8-inch cake pan and, using pot holders, turn it until the bottom and sides of the pan are coated. Set aside to cool. Any parts of the pan that are not coated with the caramel should be greased lightly with butter.

Preheat oven to 350°F.

In a small saucepan, bring the half-and-half and cream of coconut to a boil, stirring occasionally.

In a medium bowl, whisk together the eggs and egg yolks. Stirring continuously, pour the cream mixture into the eggs. Stir in the pumpkin, rum, vanilla, and allspice.

Place the cake pan in a small roasting pan. Pour the custard into the cake pan. Fill the roasting pan with enough boiling water to come halfway up the sides of the cake pan. Set in the oven and bake 35 to 45 minutes, or until a toothpick inserted in the center comes out clean. Cool and refrigerate at least 2 hours.

To serve, run a knife around the edge of the pan. Place a serving platter upside down on top of the cake pan and while holding the two firmly together, invert quickly. Serve in slices topped with the toasted coconut.

Serves 8 to 10

PUMPKIN BREAD PUDDING WITH CRANBERRY SAUCE

2 1/2 cups half-and-half

1 1/2 cups pumpkin purée

2/3 cup light brown sugar

2 eggs

1 teaspoon vanilla

1/2 teaspoon cinnamon

10 slices cinnamon raisin bread, toasted and cut into 1/2-inch pieces

1 cup (6 ounces) dried pears, cut into 1/2-inch dice

3 cups (12 ounces) cranberries

1/2 cup granulated sugar

In a medium bowl, whisk together the half-and-half, pumpkin, brown sugar, eggs, vanilla, and cinnamon. Stir in the bread and pears. Let stand 30 minutes.

Preheat oven to 350°F.

Butter an 8- by 11-inch baking pan.

Transfer the pudding mixture to the prepared pan. Bake until lightly browned and set, about 1 hour.

To make the cranberry sauce: Combine the cranberries, granulated sugar, and 1/2 cup water in a small nonreactive saucepan. Cover and bring to a simmer over medium heat. Cook until the cranberries begin to fall apart, about 10 minutes. Cool.

Serve the bread pudding warm with room temperature sauce. A scoop of pumpkin ice cream makes it even better.

Serves 8 to 10

97

THE BIGGEST PUMPKIN SHOW ON EARTH
First held in 1903 for the local farmers, the Circleville Pumpkin Show in Ohio attracts some 400,000 visitors each year. This annual festival features giant pumpkin contests, beauty pageants, and every imaginable form of cooked pumpkin. In recent years the world's largest pumpkin pie weighed 350 pounds and measured five feet in diameter! For more information call (614) 474-7000.

PUMPKIN CHEESECAKE WITH AMARETTO SOUR CREAM TOPPING

CRUST:

¾ cup graham cracker crumbs

½ cup blanched almonds, toasted and finely chopped

3 tablespoons granulated sugar

¼ cup unsalted butter, melted

FILLING:

24 ounces (three 8-ounce packages) cream cheese, softened

½ cup granulated sugar

½ cup light brown sugar

1½ cups pumpkin purée

3 eggs

2 tablespoons amaretto liqueur

1 tablespoon cornstarch

1½ teaspoons cinnamon

1 teaspoon vanilla

½ teaspoon freshly grated nutmeg

½ teaspoon ground ginger

½ teaspoon salt

TOPPING:

2 cups sour cream

2 tablespoons granulated sugar

2 tablespoons amaretto liqueur

16 whole blanched almonds, toasted, for garnish

🐾 Preheat oven to 350°F. Lightly spray a 9-inch springform cake pan with vegetable spray. Wrap the outside with aluminum foil.

To make the crust: In a bowl, combine the cracker crumbs, almonds, and sugar. Stir in the butter and press the mixture into the bottom and 1/2 inch up the side of the pan. Set in the oven and bake until the crust just begins to color, about 10 minutes.

To make the filling: In a large bowl with an electric mixer, cream together the cream cheese, granulated sugar, and brown sugar. Beat in the pumpkin, eggs, amaretto, cornstarch, cinnamon, vanilla, nutmeg, ginger, and salt until smooth.

99

(recipe continued on next page)

Pour the filling into the crust. Bake the cheesecake in the middle of the preheated oven for 50 to 55 minutes, or until the center is just set. Let cool in the pan on a rack for 5 minutes.

To make the topping: In a bowl, whisk together the sour cream, sugar, and amaretto. Spread the sour cream mixture over the top of the cheesecake and bake 5 minutes more. Let cool in the pan on a rack and then chill, covered, overnight. Remove the side of the pan and garnish the top of the cheesecake with the whole almonds.

Serves 8 to 10

BIG, BIGGER, OH MY GOD!

There's something about pumpkins that makes folk want to grow them big, real big. No North American harvest festival seems complete without a giant pumpkin contest. In 1996, Nathan and Paula Zehr of Lowville, New York, broke the thousand-pound barrier. Their 1061-pound behemoth is in the record book.

PUMPKIN ROLL CAKE WITH MAPLE CARAMEL CREAM FILLING

3/4 cup cake flour
2 teaspoons pumpkin pie spice
6 large eggs, separated
1/3 cup granulated sugar
1/3 cup light brown sugar
2/3 cup pumpkin purée
1/8 teaspoon salt

FILLING:
1 1/2 cups evaporated milk
2 egg yolks
1/3 cup maple syrup
1/3 cup brown sugar
2 tablespoons all-purpose flour
1 teaspoon vanilla
1/2 cup heavy or whipping cream

Confectioners' sugar

101

(recipe continued on next page)

Sugar and Spice

🍂 Preheat oven to 375°F.

Line a 10- by 15 1/2-inch jelly roll pan with foil, leaving a 2-inch overhang all around. Spray with nonstick vegetable cooking spray.

Sift flour and pie spice into small bowl. Using an electric mixer, beat egg yolks, granulated sugar, and brown sugar in large bowl until very thick. On low speed, beat in the pumpkin, then the flour mixture. Using clean beaters and bowl, beat the egg whites and salt until stiff but not dry. Fold egg whites into the batter. Spread evenly in the prepared pan. Bake until cake is springy to the touch and lightly browned, 10 to 12 minutes. Remove from the oven and cool 5 minutes on a wire rack, then roll up the cake lengthwise along with the foil.

To make the filling: Heat the evaporated milk in a nonreactive medium saucepan until it just comes to a boil. In a large bowl, whisk the yolks, maple syrup, brown sugar, and flour until smooth. Gradually whisk in the hot evaporated milk. Return the mixture to the

102

pan and stir over medium-low heat until it comes to a simmer and is thickened. Remove from heat and continue to whisk 1 minute longer. Stir in the vanilla. Transfer to a large bowl. Set a piece of plastic wrap directly on the surface of the custard mixture and cool to room temperature. Chill thoroughly in the refrigerator. In a separate bowl, beat the cream until it forms firm peaks and fold into the custard mixture.

To assemble the roll cake, first unroll cake. Then spread the custard filling over the cooled cake, then lifting one long end, roll the cake up, jelly roll fashion from one long side. Place seam side down on a serving platter and refrigerate at least 2 hours and up to 8 hours. Dust with the confectioners' sugar and serve.

Makes 8 to 10 servings

PUMPKIN BLINTZES WITH CARAMELIZED GINGER

BLINTZ BATTER:
3/4 cup milk
3/4 cup flour
2 eggs
1 1/2 tablespoons melted butter
2 teaspoons granulated sugar
Pinch salt

FILLING:
1 cup farmer's cheese
2/3 cup pumpkin purée
2 tablespoons chopped candied ginger
4 tablespoons light brown sugar
3 egg yolks
1 teaspoon grated orange rind
1/4 teaspoon cinnamon

2 tablespoons butter
2 tablespoons canola oil
Sour cream

🐌 *To make blintz batter:* Combine the milk, flour, eggs, butter, sugar, and salt in a blender or food processor. Blend until smooth. Pour into a small bowl, cover, and let stand 30 minutes.

Heat an 8-inch omelette or crepe pan over medium-high heat and brush lightly with butter. Remove from heat and pour in about 2½ table-spoons batter. Tilt and rotate the pan to cover the entire bottom with the batter. Return to heat, cook until the bottom is light gold and the top dry, about 1 minute. (The pancake is only cooked on one side). Remove to a piece of wax paper. Make the remaining blintzes in the same way, stacking them between layers of wax paper.

To make the filling: In a medium bowl, combine the farmer's cheese, pumpkin, ginger, sugar, egg yolks, orange rind, and cinnamon.

Spoon the filling into the center of the uncooked side of each of 8 pancakes. Fold the sides of each pancake around the filling to form a rectan-gular package. Refrigerate until ready to cook.

105

(recipe continued on next page)

Sugar and Spice

To fry the blintzes, heat the remaining butter and oil in a large skillet over moderate heat. When hot, add the blintzes, seam side down, and cook until brown and crisp on both sides. Transfer to paper towels. Serve immediately, topped by a dollop of sour cream.

Serves 4

CARVING O'LANTERNS

Pick a handsome pumpkin that's big enough for your spooky design. Using a small, sharp knife held at an angle, cut a good-sized hole either on the top or the bottom. (A hole made in the bottom makes it easier to install a candle or low-watt light bulb.) With a large metal spoon, scoop out the insides. For more elaborate designs, make a sketch on a piece of paper then transfer the pattern by taping the paper over the pumpkin and sticking a pushpin or nail through at short intervals to indicate where the cuts will go. Connect the dots, then carve. The pumpkin will be easier to handle if you start off with the little holes and work your way up to the bigger ones. A carved pumpkin usually lasts no more than five days. For a pumpkin-carving kit, contact Pumpkin Masters, Box 61456, Denver, CO 80206; (303) 722-4442.

PUMPKIN MAPLE ICE CREAM

1 cup heavy cream
1/4 cup milk
1 egg
1/4 cup light brown sugar
2/3 cup pumpkin purée
1/4 cup maple syrup
1/2 teaspoon vanilla
1/2 teaspoon cinnamon
1/8 teaspoon nutmeg
Pinch salt

In a medium saucepan, combine the cream and milk and bring to a boil. In the meantime, whisk together the egg and sugar in a large bowl. Slowly whisk in the hot milk. Stir in the pumpkin, maple syrup, vanilla, cinnamon, nutmeg, and salt. Chill thoroughly.

Freeze in an ice cream freezer according to manufacturer's directions.

Makes about 1 1/2 pints, serving 6

Sugar and Spice

CONVERSIONS

Liquid

1 tablespoon = 15 milliliters
1/2 cup = 4 fluid ounces = 125 milliliters
1 cup = 8 fluid ounces = 250 milliliters

Dry

1/4 cup = 4 tablespoons = 2 ounces = 60 grams
1 cup = 1/2 pound = 8 ounces = 250 grams

Flour

1/2 cup = 60 grams
1 cup = 4 ounces = 125 grams

Temperature

400 degrees F = 200 degrees C = gas mark 6
375 degrees F = 190 degrees C = gas mark 5
350 degrees F = 175 degrees C = gas mark 4

Miscellaneous

2 tablespoons butter = 1 ounce = 30 grams
1 inch = 2.5 centimeters
all purpose flour = plain flour
baking soda = bicarbonate of soda
brown sugar= demerara sugar
confectioners' sugar = icing sugar
heavy cream = double cream
molasses= black treacle
raisins = sultanas
rolled oats = oat flakes
semisweet chocolate = plain chocolate
sugar= caster sugar